BLUEPRINT

English Key Stag
Copymasters

Jim Fitzsimmons

Rhona Whiteford

Stanley Thornes (Publishers) Ltd

BLUEPRINTS – HOW TO GET MORE INFORMATION

Blueprints is an expanding series of practical teacher's ideas books and photocopiable resources for use in primary schools. Books are available for every Key Stage of every core and foundation subject, as well as for an ever widening range of other primary needs. **Blueprints** are carefully structured around the demands of National Curriculum but may be used successfully by schools and teachers not following the National Curriculum in England and Wales.

Blueprints provide:

- Total National Curriculum coverage
- Hundreds of practical ideas
- Books specifically for the Key Stage you teach
- Flexible resources for the whole school or for individual teachers
- Excellent photocopiable sheets – ideal for assessment, SATs and children's work profiles
- Supreme value.

Books may be bought by credit card over the telephone and information obtained on (0242) 228888. Alternatively, photocopy and return this FREEPOST form to join our mailing list. We will mail you regularly with information on new and existing titles.

Please add my name to the BLUEPRINTS mailing list. *Photocopiable*

Name _____

Address_____

_____

_____

Postcode_____

To: Marketing Services Dept., Stanley Thornes Publishers, FREEPOST (GR 782), Cheltenham, Glos. GL53 1BR

First published in 1991 by:
Stanley Thornes (Publishers) Ltd
Ellenborough House
Wellington Street
CHELTENHAM GL50 1YD

Reprinted 1992
Reprinted 1993 (twice)

British Library Cataloguing in Publication Data
Fitzsimmons, Jim
  Blueprints English: key stage 1: Copymasters.
  I. Title   II. Whiteford, Rhona
  372.6
  ISBN 0-7487-1171-6

Typeset by Kalligraphic Design Ltd, Horley, Surrey.
Printed in Great Britain at The Bath Press, Avon.

CONTENTS

In this book there are 122 photocopiable copymasters linked to many of the activities in the Teacher's Resource Book. Where the copymasters are referred to in the text of the Teacher's Resource Book there are instructions on how to use them. They are referred to by number in the Teacher's Resource Book by this symbol ⬠ . The copymasters reinforce and extend activities in the Teacher's Resource Book and provide opportunities to record activities and results in an organised way. When the children have completed these copymasters they can be added to workfiles or used as exemplar material in pupil profiles. You may also wish to use completed copymasters as a resource for your assessments.

Making things

My name is

I played with

I made a

How does it end?

Pick a person

Little Bo-peep

Simple Simon

The Knave of Hearts

Mary Mary Quite Contrary

Little Miss Muffett

Little Jack Horner

Old King Cole

Miss Polly had a dolly

The Grand Old Duke of York

Draw a most unusual creature

Our game

Step by step

My favourite TV programme

Favourite story

1 Fairy stories

2 Adventure stories

3 Everyday stories

4 Super-heroes

5 Animal stories

6 Ghost stories

7 Machine stories

8 Toys stories

Things I like to do

tennis

swimming

cycling

camping

watching TV

eating my favourite food

football

painting

helping Mum/Dad

day trips

going to the park

going to the cinema

Comic strip

Ugly mugs

My story

Beginning

Middle

End

Can you write your name?

Colour the child's hair the same as yours.
Colour the jumper the same as yours.

Choosing books

My favourite things

My favourite character

My favourite topic

Looking after the plants

Looking after the pets

Looking after the classroom

Clothes

Draw a line to join each word to the
right part of the picture.

scarf

coat

hat

gloves

zip

trousers

boots

Our classroom

Draw a line to join each word to the right part of the picture.

window

door

Anna   Lee

Michael   Hayley

Paul   Sean

Kevin   Cherie

trays

table

chair

bookshelf

carpet

blackboard

box

Initial letters

C21

Look at the pictures. Say the sounds.

a	b	c	d	e
f	g	h	i	j
k	l	m	n	o
p	q	r	s	t
u	v	w	x	y	z

fox

Recognising sounds

Colour each letter balloon in turn when you know the sound the letter makes.

Find the letter

Look at the picture. Guess the word.
Fill in the letter for the missing sound.

_ rrow	_ oat	_ ake
_ og	_ lephant	_ ish
_ ate	_ at	_ nsect

a	b	c	d	e	f	g	h	i

Find the letter

Look at the picture. Guess the word.
Fill in the letter for the missing sound.

_eans	_ey	_eg
_ittens	_et	_rang-utan
_an	_uack	_attle

| j | k | l | m | n | o | p | q | r |

Find the letter

Look at the picture. Guess the word.
Fill in the letter for the missing sound.

_un

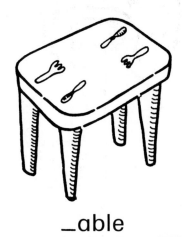

_able

_mbrella

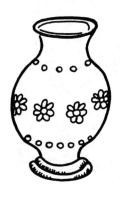

_ase

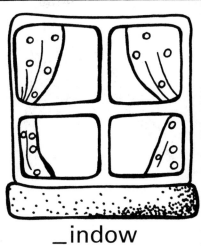

_indow

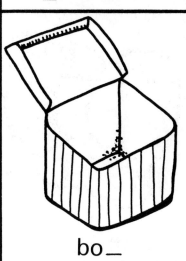

bo_

_acht

_ebra

a b c d e
f g h i j k
l m n o p
q r s t u
v w x y z

s t u v w x y z

I spy

Surprise!

Look at the pictures and try to tell the story.

One day a strange seed appeared in Don's garden.

The three wishes

Read the story and try to put in the missing words.

This is a little  called Angela.

One day she met a  with a magic

The pixie gave Angela wishes.

The three wishes

Angela wished for a

Next she wished for a

Then she wished she lived in an

Draw what you
would wish for.

Who am I?

Read each sentence in turn. Try to guess the missing word. Write the word.

I am a  boy.

I am a  girl.

I am a  mum.

I am a  dad.

I am a  baby.

Draw a line to join each word to the right person.

Go for a ride

C29

Read each sentence and say the name for the picture. Copy the name for the picture.

Here is a  bus.

_____

Here is a  boat.

_____

Here is a  car.

_____

Here is a  bicycle.

_____

Here is a  train.

_____

Things on the table

Read each sentence and say the name for the picture. Try to copy the sentence.

This is a  knife.

This is a  fork.

This is a  spoon.

This is a 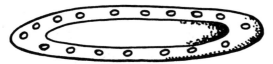 plate.

Draw your favourite meal.

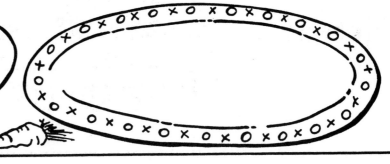

In the garden

Find the missing word hidden in the flower.
Write it in the sentence. Then copy the sentence.

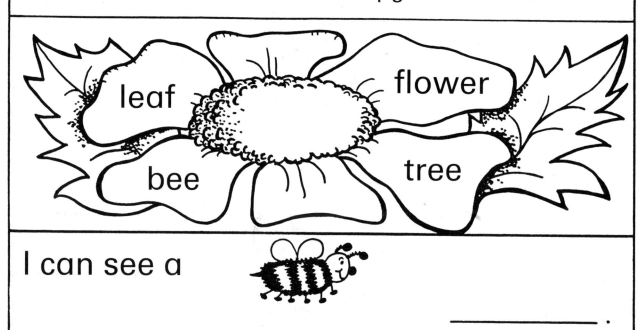

leaf

flower

bee

tree

I can see a

_____.

I can see a

_____

I can see a

_____

I can see a

_____.

What are they saying?

Read and then write.

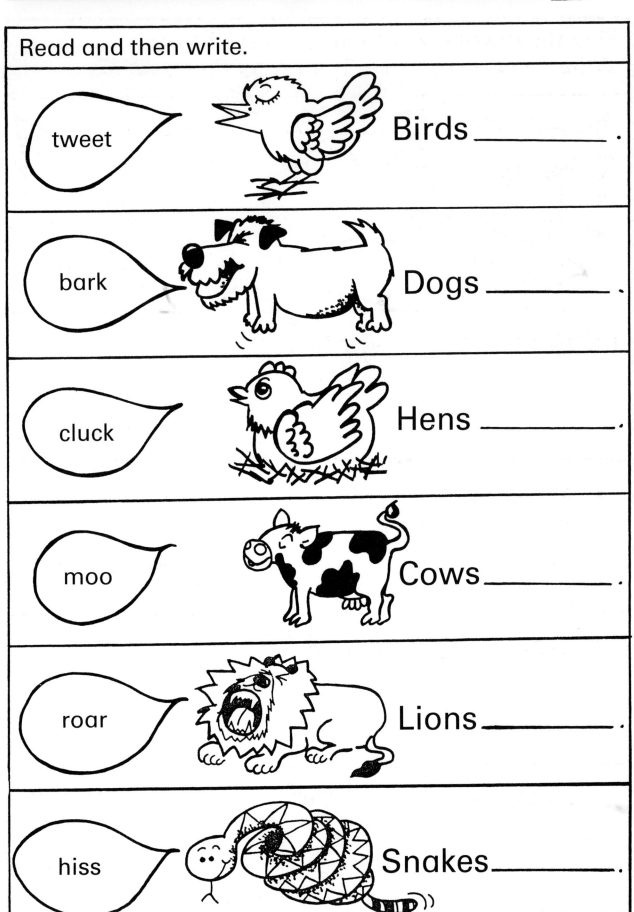

tweet	Birds _____.
bark	Dogs _____.
cluck	Hens _____.
moo	Cows _____.
roar	Lions _____.
hiss	Snakes _____.

The fairground

Read the sentences to colour the picture.

Colour the sky blue.

Colour the balloons red.

Colour the sun orange.

Colour a stall yellow and red.

Colour the grass green.

Guess what

Read each sentence. Say the missing word.
Use the picture as a clue.

I swim.

I have fins and scales.

I am a

I can fly.

I have feathers.

I am a

I am like a horse.

I have stripes.

I am a

Can you see?

Find the correct ending.
Draw a line to finish the sentence.

The boat is sailing   caught a fish.

The woman is standing   the river.

The train is   on the water.

The boy has   in the doorway.

Two fish are in   on the bridge.

Can you read this?

Read the word. Colour the picture and write the word underneath.

doll

_____

car

_____

game

_____

teddy

_____

Matching words and pictures

Draw a line to match each picture with the right word.

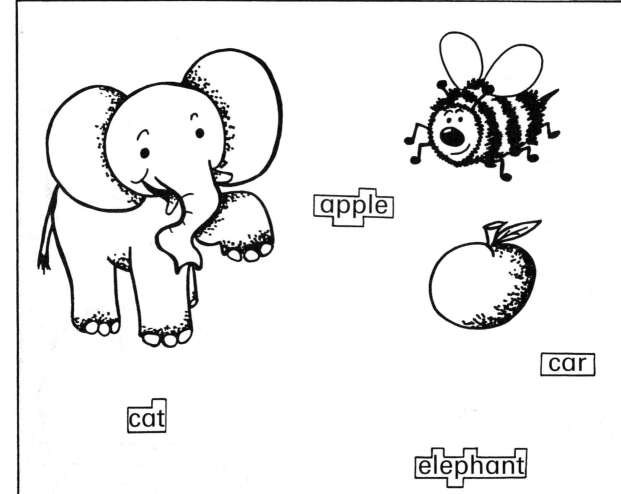

apple

car

cat

elephant

bee

Matching words

Match the words. Colour the partners the same.

Matching sounds

Ring the letter that has the same sound as the first one in each row.

a	h	i	p	a	l
b	g	b	o	t	x
c	h	i	c	p	u
d	j	n	q	v	d
e	e	k	r	z	l
f	m	f	s	w	y
g	j	o	x	t	g

Make pairs

Match the words
Colour each
pair the
same colour.

g

m

d

g

r

i

q

r

d

q

i

m

Which one?

Say the sound. Circle the thing that starts with that sound.

s	   
t	   
u	  
w	  
p	  

Which sound?

C42

Look at the picture. Say the word.
Circle the sound that starts the word.

	m u p c v
	i h a l n
	o c b f q
	h b e f g
	t x k z h
	d j r s y

Start the word

Choose the word

Look at the picture.
Say the word.
Circle the right word.

tree   house   yacht

ball   net   kettle

flowers   trees   bee

toad   snake   bird

Finish the sentence

C45

Write the missing word. What sound does the word begin with?

Here is a _ _ _ .

bat
dog
log

I am a _ _ _ _ _ .

door
clown
wasp

This is a _ _ _ _ _ .

car
lorry
ship

Here is a _ _ _ _ _ _ .

roof
floor
window

Down on the farm

Draw a line under the correct word.

The farmer's wife is driving the

digger
car
tractor

The farmer is feeding the

child
ducks
hens

The little dog is playing with a

ball
doll
girl

Playtime

Draw a line under the correct word.

Who is on the branch?	boy	frog
Who is on the fence?	girl	boy
Who has two babies?	sun	cow
Who looks over the hill?	frog	sun
Who has the bat?	girl	squirrel
Who kicks the leaves?	frog	boy

The magic balloons

Look at the pictures. Tell the story.
Draw what happens next.

Footprints in the mud

Susan was sitting reading when suddenly there was a crash outside.

She looked out and saw two giant footprints.

What happened next?

Creepy Castle

John was visiting a big castle.

As he walked through one of the rooms he saw a ghost.

What happened next?

A house of sweets

The house was not very big. The walls were made of icing-sugar decorated with chocolate drops at each corner.

The door was made of a bar of milk chocolate.

The windows were made of barley-sugar and all around the window frames were large pink pear-drops.

The roof was covered with swirls of marshmallow, and all along the top of it were rows of tiny silver balls.

In the garden there were lollipop trees and dolly-mixture flowers, with a lemonade pond.

Speak like me

Match the words to the speaker. Then say the words in the sort of voice the speaker might have.

troll

Mummy, I want my bottle.

giant

Fee fi fo fum,
I smell the blood of an Englishman.

baby

You look like a good dinner.

mouse

Take me to your leader.

alien

That does not compute.
Repeat instructions.

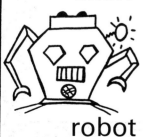

robot

Oh, for a delicious piece of cheese.

Turning points

Name of story _____

Characters _____

Place _____

_____

The story was about _____

_____

_____

_____

Things changed when . . .

What will they do?

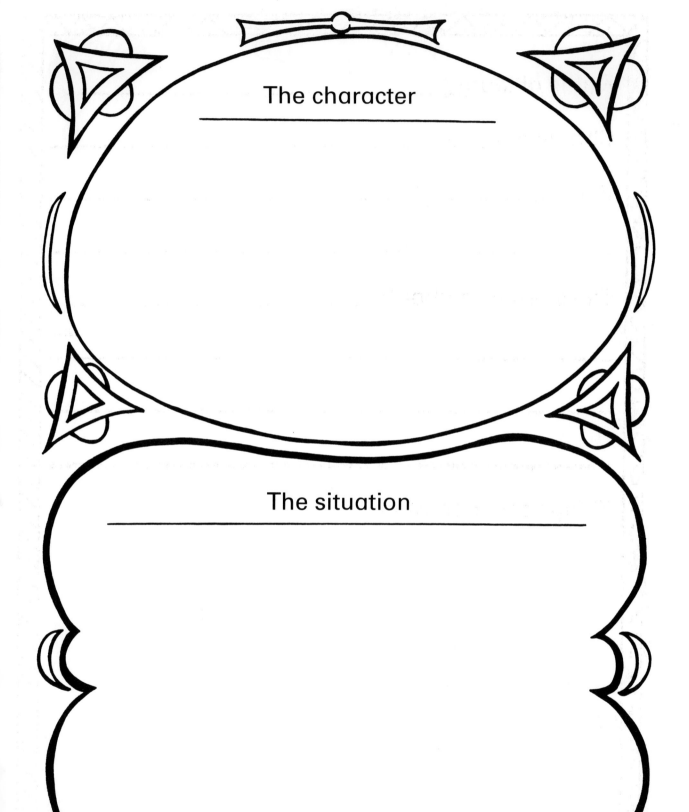

The character
_____

The situation
_____

Jim and the beans

C55

At the beginning

The story ends with

My story

It all started when

In the end

Looking for information

Title of topic_____

_____

Where will I find the book?_____

_____

Which shelf? _____

_____

What do I need to know?_____

_____

_____

_____

Notes _____

_____

_____

_____

_____

_____

We want fancy clothes

Sarah and Adam want their clothes decorated.
Finish Sarah's stripes and Adam's spots.

Adventure under the sea

Diver Dan sees a lot of strange things underwater.
Draw some more shells, seaweed and fish.

My story

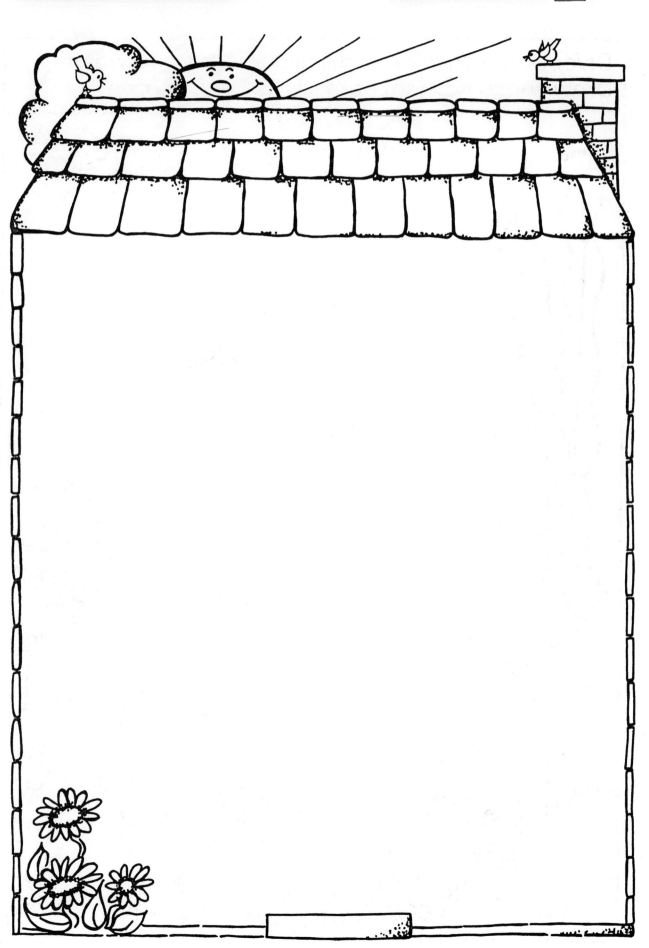

My pets

Shopping

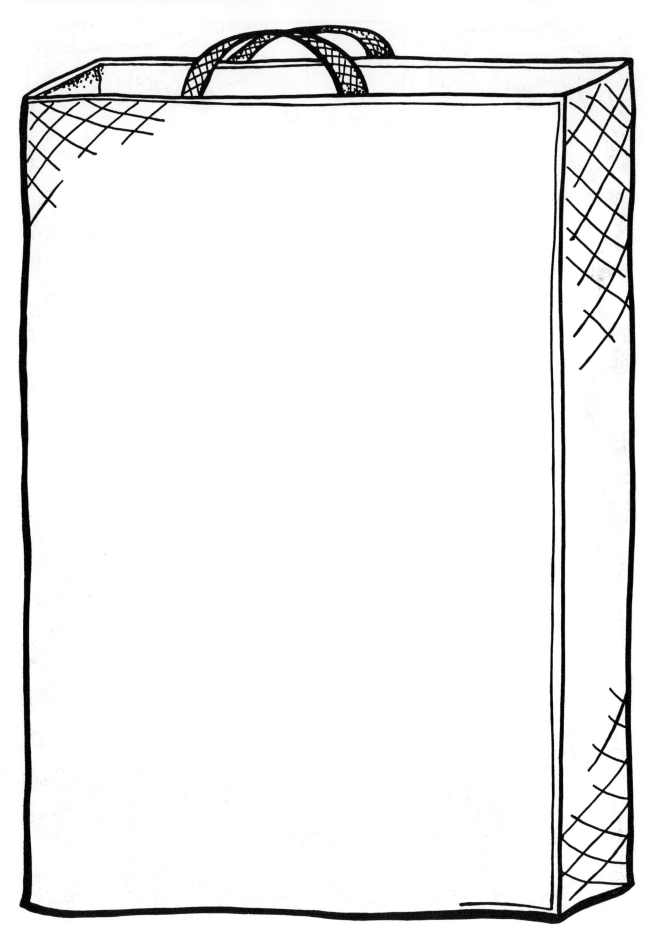

I am

I can

I like

What will he say?

Telling words

What are these things like? Pick a word for each.

gorgeous glittering wobbly fantastic jolly fierce

jelly

hairy bean

giant

jewelled ring

smile

Getting ready for school

Storyboard

characters	place
time	**main events**
opening	**ending**

Characters

Name		
Type		
Age		
male		female

Looks

Behaviour

Openings

It was snowing heavily and the night was dark. Soon the fields were covered with a blanket of snow. It was very quiet.

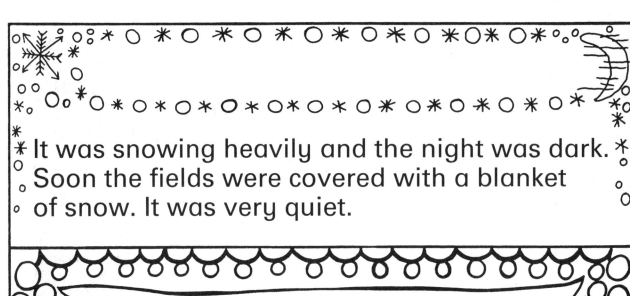

The room was brightly lit and full of all the colours of the rainbow.

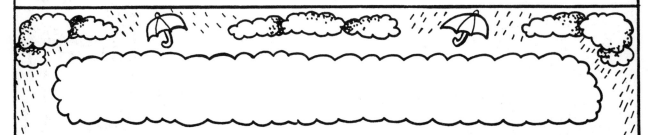

One cold afternoon the clouds were grey and rain began to fall on the pavements and roofs.

Slowly and quietly the door opened.

Ways to start a story

Once upon a time . . .

One day . . .

In a land far away . . .

Last year . . .

One day I am going to . . .

It was a dark, dark night . . .

Not long ago . . .

A long, long time ago . . .

One bright sunny morning . . .

Every night . . .

It happened like this . . .

I must tell you about . . .

Ways to end a story

. . . and they all lived happily ever after.

. . . and that was the end of that.

It had all been a dream.

. . . and so goodnight to everyone.

They were all as happy as could be.

So they walked off together.

It had ended, at long last.

The end.

Goodnight.

The snowman

The castle

Lists

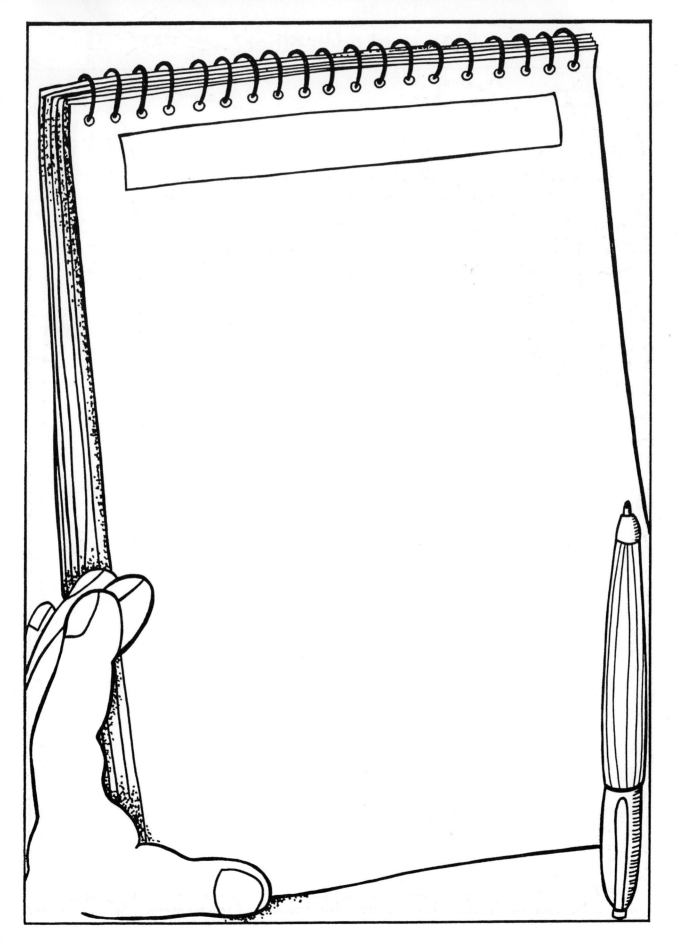

Speech bubbles

What are they saying to each other?

Invitation

invites

to a

on the

at ◯ o'clock

to be held at

Rumplestiltskin

once there was a miller who had a beautiful and clever daughter he was so proud that he boasted to the king that she could spin straw into gold can she now muttered the king and took her away to his palace

he locked her up with a pile of straw and a spinning wheel and told her to spin the straw into gold or she would die what can I do she wept just then a strange little man appeared and said he could make the gold in return for her ring this happened three times until the daughter had nothing to give this time the little man made her promise to give him her child when she was queen thinking this would never happen she promised

the king had so much gold he was happy and married the girl soon the new queen had a baby and the magic man came to claim it guess my name or I take it he cried she tried but failed a servant heard him singing his name in the forest and told the queen when she asked is rumplestiltskin your name he was so shocked he roared with rage and disappeared for ever the king and queen were happy

Joining sentences

Spring into action and use these words to join the pairs of sentences. Write the new sentence underneath.

before so because after but when

John ran to school.   He was still late.

We had supper.   We went to bed.

I was chopping wood.   I cut my finger.

It was very dark.   I could not see.

The boy was late.   He missed the bus.

Descriptions

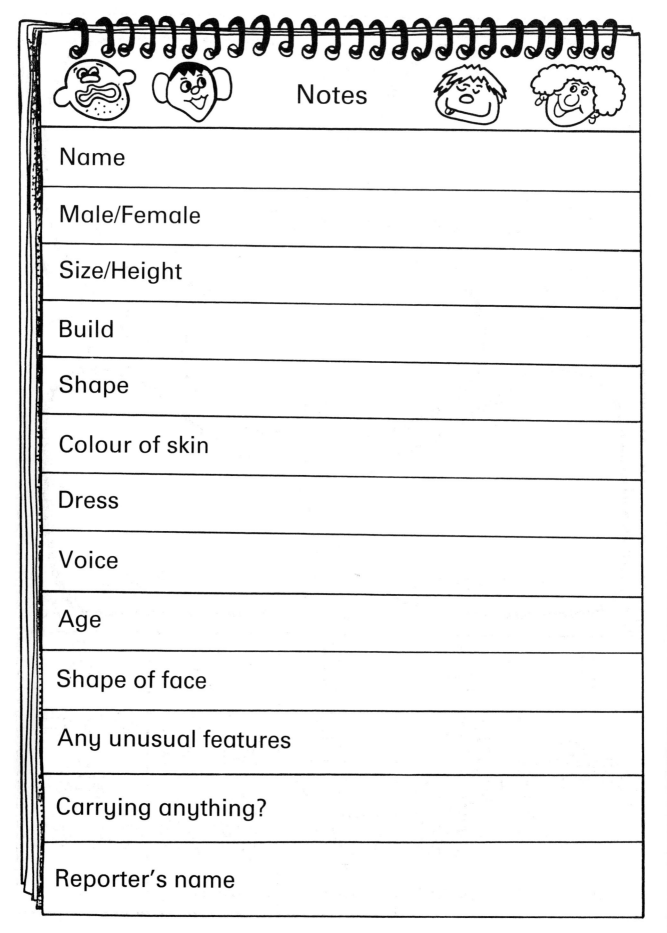

Notes

Name

Male/Female

Size/Height

Build

Shape

Colour of skin

Dress

Voice

Age

Shape of face

Any unusual features

Carrying anything?

Reporter's name

Numbers, letters and pictures

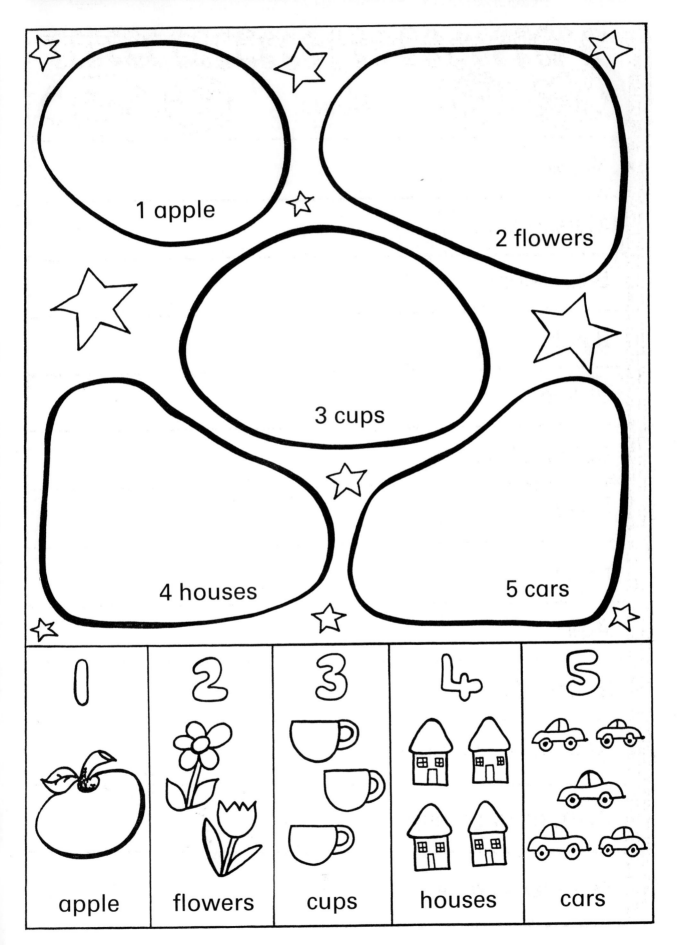

Find the letter

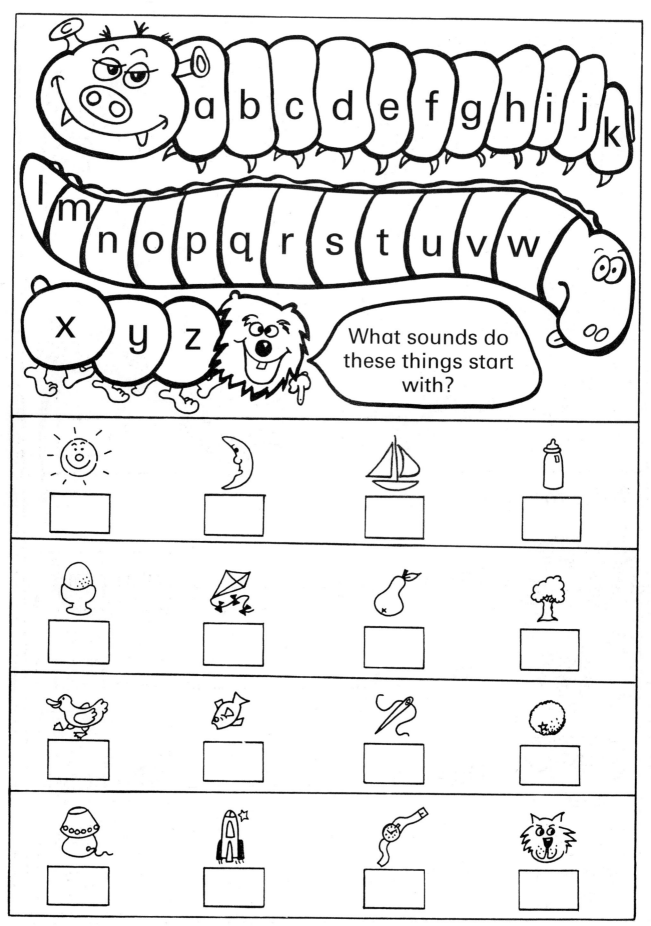

Take your pick

Write the missing letters.

do ☐   ha ☐   ma ☐   pi ☐

su ☐   zi ☐   pa ☐   lo ☐

Write the correct words.

This is a _____ | bun | bus |

This is a _____ | cap | cat |

This is a _____ | cub | cup |

This is a _____ | fish | dish |

Word patterns

C83

Finish the words with the same sound patterns.

bib   lid   net   tub   hill

n _____   d _____   g _____   c _____   f _____

r _____   h _____   m _____   h _____   t _____

f _____   k _____   p _____   r _____   m _____

Write the words.

_ _ _ _   _ _ _ _   _ _ _ _   _ _ _ _   _ _ _ _

  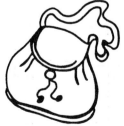  

_ _ _ _   _ _ _ _   _ _ _ _   _ _ _ _   _ _ _ _

Word sheet

Look/cover/write	Check ✔	Write again

Blends at the beginning

Put the first sound in each word.

Blends at the end

Colour the words that end in **nd** in red.
Colour the words that end in **ng** in yellow.

ring

lend

long

wind

hand

bend

sing

sand

grand

bang

ng

nd

Write **nt** words in me.

Write **st** words in my tum.

pest

sent

mint   pant

tent

rest

last

bent

hint

nest

lost

must

dent   cost

nt

st

One sound from two

Sometimes **ch** is at the beginning of a word.
Sometimes it is at the end.

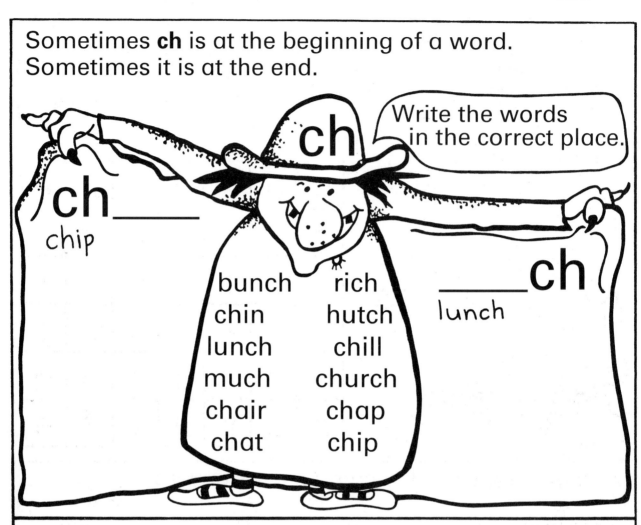

Write the words
in the correct place.

ch___

chip

ch

_____ch

lunch

bunch   rich
chin   hutch
lunch   chill
much   church
chair   chap
chat   chip

Write the words that start with **sh** in the little fish.

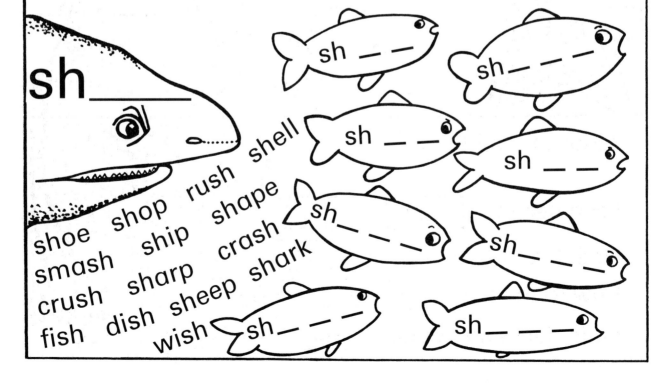

sh___

shoe shop rush shell
smash ship shape
crush sharp crash
fish dish sheep shark
wish

sh _ _ _

sh _ _ _

sh _ _ _

sh _ _ _

sh_____

sh_____

sh_____

sh_____

One sound from two – more examples

kn

Look at the sound box.
Colour the words
which start with **kn**.

a	b	k	n	o	w	e
c	k	n	e	e	d	f
k	n	i	t	g	h	i
k	i	k	n	e	w	j
m	k	n	o	t	o	n
p	q	k	n	i	f	e

Add the first sound to complete each word.

qu
_ _ een
_ _ ack
_ _ ick
_ _ iet

ph
_ _ ilip
_ _ one
_ _ oto
_ _ antom

Colour the right word.

I can use the | bone | phone |

One, two, three, pat your | knee | tree |

Bow to the king and | stream | queen |

Little ducks say quack | back | quack |

ee and oo

ee   oo

Add the right sound to each word.

r _ _ f	m _ _ n	f _ _ t	tr _ _ s	ball _ _ n	t _ _ t	b _ _

ee

Fill in the missing sounds. Write the words on the list.

tr e e

kn _ _
bl _ _ p
cr _ _ p
gr _ _ n
sw _ _ t

n _ _ d
s _ _
w _ _ k

tree

oo

Fill in the missing letters.

1 Animals are kept in a _ oo.

2 The _ oo _ shines at night.

3 I love to eat nice _ oo _ .

4 A _ oo _ goes on top of a house.

5 _ oo _ s go on your feet.

6 I can dive into a _ oo _ .

Building blocks

ea	ea	
h<u>ea</u>d	n<u>ea</u>t	

ow	ow	oa
d<u>ow</u>n	sn<u>ow</u>	

oi	oy	ou	ay

ai	a_e	o_e	i_e	u_e

The alphabet

Aa	Bb	Cc
Dd	Ee	Ff
Gg	Hh	Ii
Jj	Kk	Ll
Mm	Nn	Oo

The alphabet

C91b

P p	Q q	R r
S s	T t	U u
V v	W w	X x
Y y	Z z	

A B C D E F G H I J K L M N O P Q R S T U V W X Y Z
a b c d e f g h i j k l m n o p q r s t u v w x y z

Scribbles

The kittens are playing with Mum's wool.
Draw the mess they have made. Use a different
colour for each ball.

Join the strings

Colour the balloons and draw the strings.

Stop

Stop all the vehicles at the traffic lights.

One, two, three, four

Draw the sails on the boats
and colour them in.

Take the little dog home

Start at the dot at the top and take the dog to the kennel. Try to stay inbetween the lines with your pencil.

Patterns

Draw the patterns on the blanket.

Matching

Colour the picture which is the same as the first one in each row.

Find a way

Help the children to find their picnic.

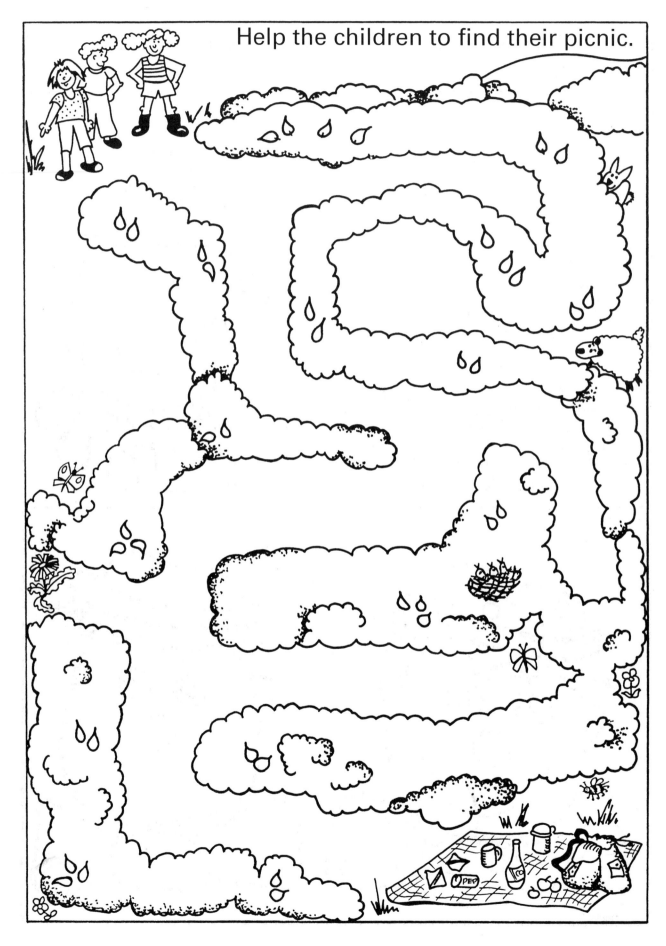

Complete the picture

Make the second clown in each pair the same as the first.

Tracing pictures

Tracing pictures

Tracing c, o, a

cat

c c c c c

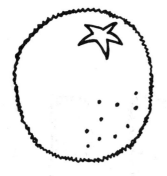

orange

o o o o o

apple

a a a a a

Tracing d, g, q

dog

d d d d d

girl

g g g g g

queen

q q q q q

Tracing l, i, j

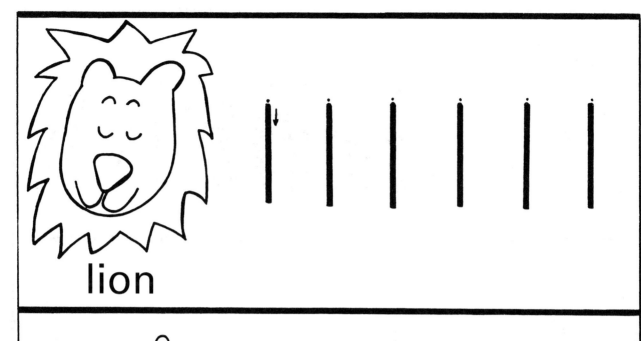

lion

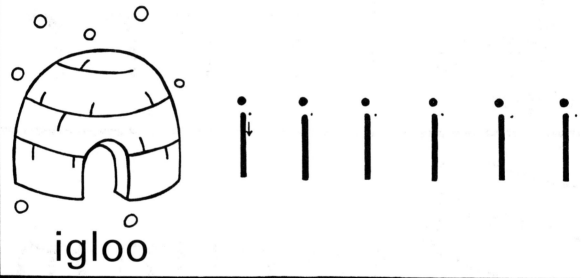

igloo

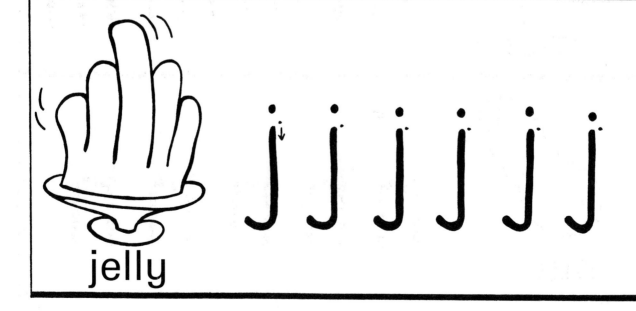

jelly

heart

h h h h h

rope

r r r r r

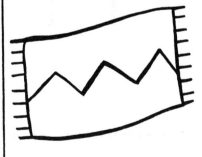

mat

m m m m m

nut

n n n n n

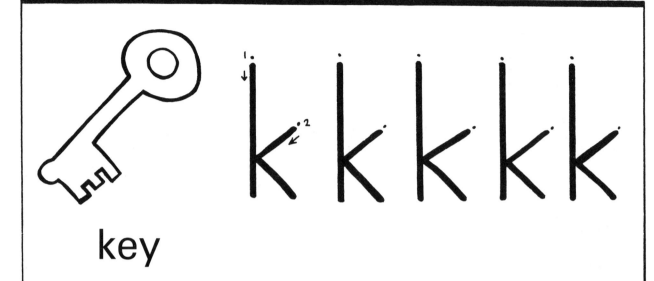

key

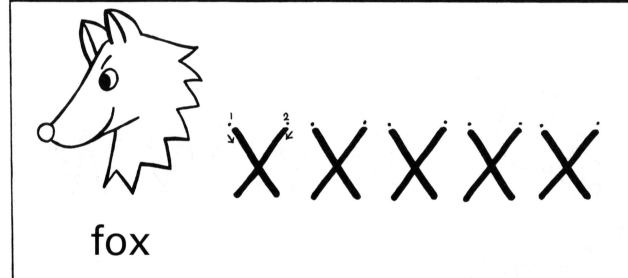

fox

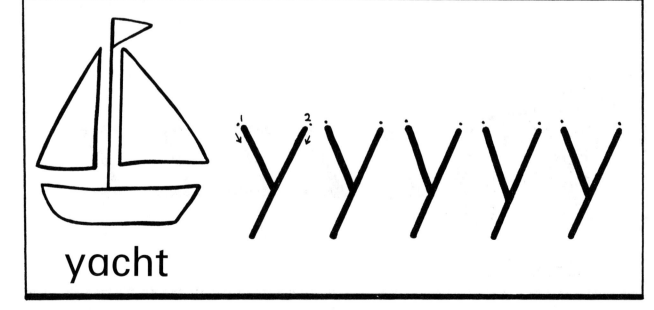

yacht

V V V V V

violin

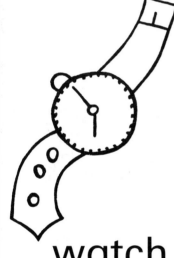

W W W W W

watch

Z Z Z Z Z

zebra

flag

toes

umbrella

yawn

Tracing p, b, s, e

pig

p p p p p

balloon

b b b b b

snake

s s s s s

egg

e e e e e

Patterns

Capital letters

Finish these rows.

A A A

M M M

V V V

W W W

Y Y Y

X X X

H H H

I I I

Copy this underneath.

A W N V M Y X A W N V M Y X A W N

Capital patterns

/B/B/B/B/B/B/B/B/B/B/B/B/B

Finish these patterns.

GCGCG

BDBDB

EFEFE

ZNZNZ

IRIRI

PLPLPL

KBKBK

Now do some of your own.

The alphabet

A B C D E F G H I J K L

a b c d e f g h i j k l

M N O P Q R S T U V

m n o p q r s t u v

W X Y Z

w x y z

A B C D E F G H I J K L

M N O P Q R S T U V

W X Y Z

Using capital letters

Here are some street name-plates.
The painter has written them all
with small letters.
Rewrite them in capitals.

cross st

acacia ave

end lane

Write your own name and
address here.

It's for
yoo hooo!

Mr. B. Messy,
4 Untidy Street,
Tattyville,
Dumpshire.

Write these city names on the road signs in capital
letters.

Edinburgh	London	Dublin	Glasgow
Manchester	Leeds	Cardiff	Newcastle

Up and down

bpbpbp

tjtjtjtj

ykykyky

fjfjfjfjf

gfgfgfg

hqhqhq

bgbgbg

dpdpdpd

dydydyd

Writing practice